Different is NOT BAD
Different is the WORLD

A Book About Disabilities

by Sally L. Smith
illustrated by Ben Booz

Copyright © 1994 by Sally L. Smith
All rights reserved.

ISBN # 1-57035-030-2

Cover artwork and illustrations by Ben Booz
Text layout and cover design by Susan Krische
Edited by Jami Leutheuser

Published and
Distributed by:

Sopris West

1140 Boston Avenue • Longmont, CO 80501 • (303) 651-2829

Introduction

The purpose of this book is to help children (grades 2-6) realize that being "different" is O.K.; in fact, it makes people more interesting and the world a better place. This book is intended to help children with disabilities feel better about themselves. Plus, children without disabilities will see that people who are different have different ways of accomplishing everyday tasks, but people can do almost anything in their own way. The message is: Respect and prize diversity!

For Teachers, Parents, and Other Adults

When reading this book to children, have them discuss each set of drawings, then point out that each set is very different, all good, each of value (each important).

When seeing that something may not work, when it is in the wrong place, or doesn't fit, elicit from the children, "Why not?" Pages 7 and 11 talk about "a nuisance," which can be interpreted to be "a bother," "an obstacle," or "a pain."

On pages 14-17, when discussing what each person does well, help the children reflect on what one or two things they do best and what activities cause them difficulties.

Pages 21 and 28 discuss people's patchwork quilts of abilities and nuisances. Talk frankly about your own strengths and weaknesses with the children. For example, "I read and write well, but I've never been good at sports or math." Then ask the children to discuss theirs.

After reading the whole book, demonstrate visually to the children how you might fill in a patchwork quilt of your "CAN DOs" and "CAN'T DOs." Then have the children color and label (or dictate, if they can't read or write) their own unique quilts. On the next page is a sample quilt you can photocopy for this purpose.

You will need to read this book to the children several times and help them to look at all the pictures very carefully. Children may then be given the book to read on their own if they are able, or to use the audio tape (available from the publisher) to listen to the book being read. It is hoped that with the audio tape they will point to each of the drawings, look at them in detail (time has been provided on the tape before each "page turn indicator" for the children to examine the pictures), talk about them, and reflect on the fact that differences are O.K.

Color your own quilt of **CAN DOs** and **CAN'T DOs**.

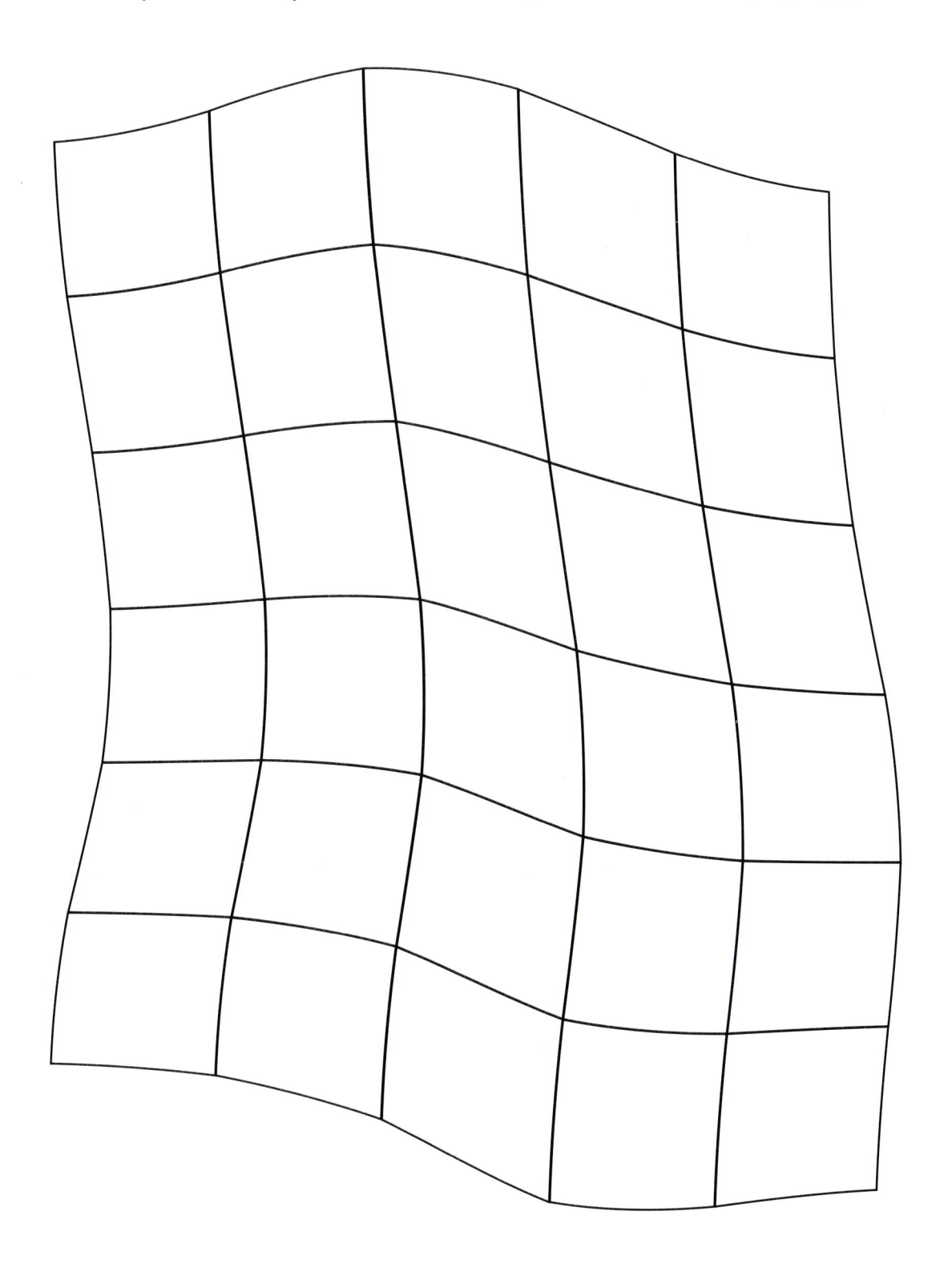

Each **DIFFERENT**. Each of **VALUE**.

The world has many different countries, each with its own holidays.

VERY DIFFERENT,

ALL GOOD,

each of VALUE.

People all over the world live in **HOUSES**.

Many kinds of houses,

VERY DIFFERENT,

each of VALUE.

2

They are

ALL

GOOD

even though

some of them may not work

when they are in the **WRONG PLACE**.

People all over the world like to DRIVE many kinds of vehicles,

VERY DIFFERENT,

each of VALUE.

They are

ALL GOOD.

But sometimes they don't work

when they are in the **WRONG PLACE**.

All over the world, people wear **CLOTHES**.
They are all **VERY DIFFERENT**,
but each of **VALUE**.

They are
ALL GOOD.

But sometimes they are a **NUISANCE**.

They don't **FIT**,

they are in the **WRONG PLACE**.

7

Everybody in the world has a FACE and every face is DIFFERENT.

THEY ARE ALL GOOD.

Yours is, too!

Faces show **FEELINGS**.

FEELINGS are all **O.K.**

But sometimes they are expressed at the

WRONG TIME, in the **WRONG PLACE**.

People everywhere have different kinds of **BODIES**,

VERY DIFFERENT,

each of VALUE.

They are
ALL GOOD.

But sometimes they are a
NUISANCE
when they don't FIT,
when they are in the WRONG SPACE.

11

Sometimes differences in our bodies mean that we must
DO THINGS DIFFERENTLY.

People who are blind can read with their fingers instead of their eyes.

They may use a special cane to find their way.

People who are deaf often talk with their hands, using sign language.

A person who is physically disabled can do lots of things in a wheelchair.

12

Physical differences are **NOT BAD**, but they require **SPECIAL HELP**, like

"talking books" on tape

an interpreter

speech therapy

ramps for wheelchairs

13

Everybody has a **BRAIN** that is different, **VERY DIFFERENT**, but each of **VALUE**.

This man's brain is good at **SCIENCE** but not at writing poetry. For him, writing is difficult.

This girl's brain is good at **MUSIC** but not at learning languages. For her, language is confusing.

This boy is good at **PLANNING SPACE** (like architects) but not at reading. For him, reading is puzzling.

Brains are **ALL GOOD**, but brains are usually not good at *everything*. Sometimes brains force people to find **DIFFERENT WAYS** to do things. Look at all the different ways of making a *book report*.

There is a written report

a diorama

a film

an illustration

an oral report

and a flip book.

15

All of us are **GOOD** at **DIFFERENT** things, **VERY DIFFERENT**, but each of **VALUE**.

DIFFERENT

often means a

SPECIAL ABILITY.

REMEMBER:

Different is NOT BAD

Different is NOT LAZY

NOT DUMB

NOT WEIRD

Different is NOT STUPID

NOT UGLY

NOT DORKY

Different is NOT NERDY

Different **can be** a **NUISANCE** when you

can't **READ**,

can't **CONCENTRATE**,

don't know **UP** from **DOWN** or **RIGHT** from **LEFT**,

can't **SPEAK CLEARLY**,

or can't understand **NUMBERS**.

The NUISANCES can make you feel

DEPRESSED

ANGRY   GUILTY   NO GOOD

like wanting to HIDE

from shame,

like PICKING on others,

OR

nuisances can make you feel

MORE DETERMINED THAN EVER to succeed.

DIFFERENT

often makes you feel like a patchwork quilt

of abilities and nuisances,

of **CAN DOs**

and **CAN'T DOs**.

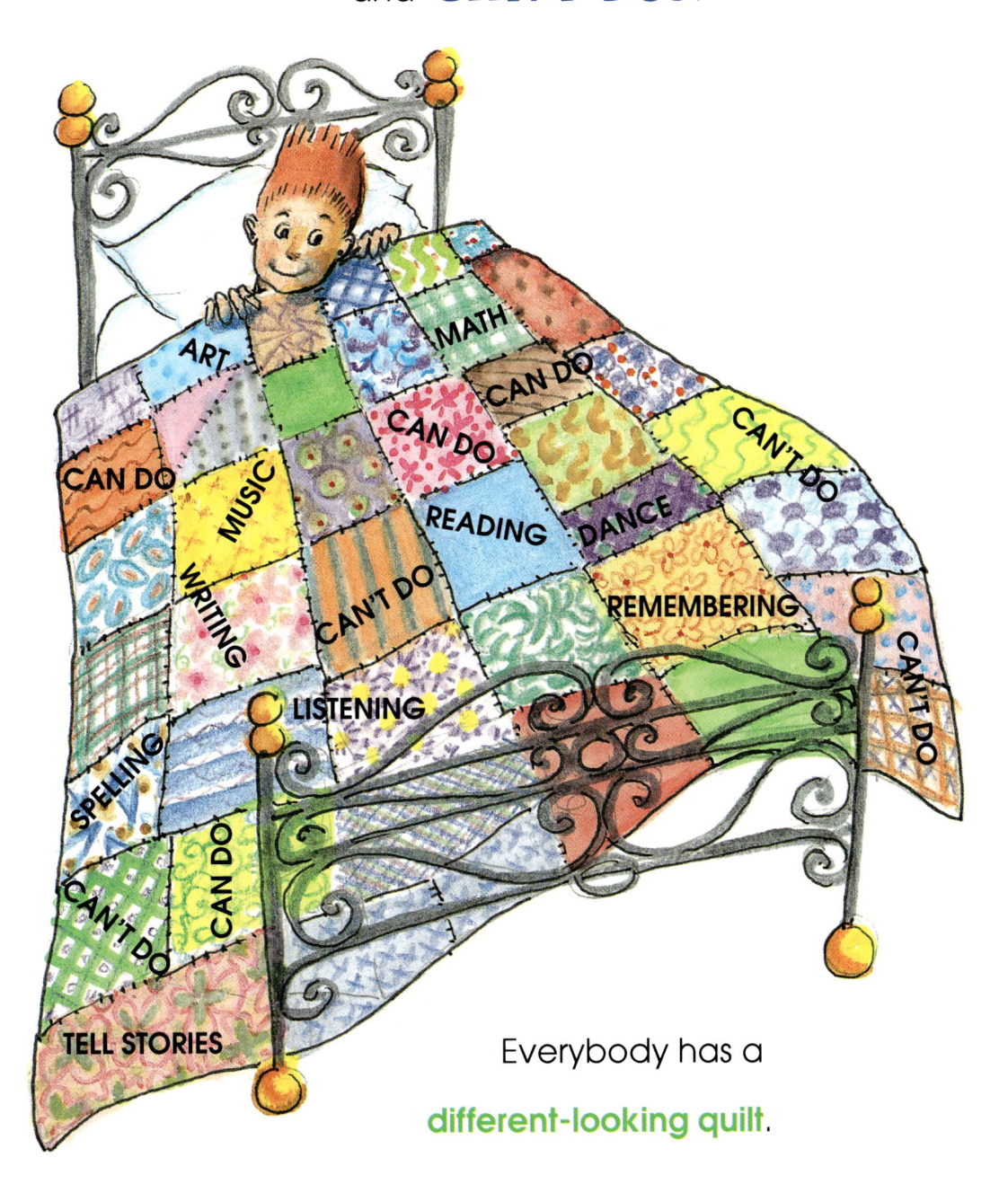

Everybody has a

different-looking quilt.

THEY ARE ALL GOOD.

People who have difficulty

LEARNING IN SCHOOL

may need special help, like

equipment

a tutor

different activities

or a special class.

College students with learning disabilities often have

a special class,

different equipment,

and **THEY SUCCEED**.

They learn **HOW to** get along differently and they learn to feel **GOOD** about being **DIFFERENT**, to feel **GOOD** about **THEMSELVES**.

Some **famous people** in history lived in different **COUNTRIES**, had different **HOUSES**, **CLOTHES**, **FACES**, **BODIES**, and **BRAINS**, **ABILITIES** and **DISABILITIES**. For example

Thomas Edison, who invented the electric light bulb, was learning disabled.

Ludwig von Beethoven composed some of his greatest music while deaf.

Auguste Rodin, a French sculptor who carved "The Thinker," was thought to be learning disabled.

Franklin D. Roosevelt, a President of the United States, was physically disabled.

Helen Keller earned a Master's degree and became a writer while deaf and blind.

Nelson Rockefeller, a Vice President of the United States, was learning disabled.

Leonardo da Vinci, the Italian artist who painted the "Mona Lisa," was thought to be learning disabled.

General George Patton, a great strategist who helped to win World War II, was learning disabled.

They had to work **HARDER** and **LONGER**. They had to make the **MOST** of what they did **WELL**.

There are also lots of people who are **NOT FAMOUS**, who have great abilities as well as disabilities, who enjoy **HAPPY, SUCCESSFUL LIVES**.

the head of a bicycle factory

a teacher

a disc jockey

an earth mover

a soldier

26

a dental assistant

a boutique manager

an optician

a firefighter

a hair stylist

27

People need to know their own **STRENGTHS** and **WEAKNESSES**.

They need to make their **OWN** quilts of **CAN DOs** and **CAN'T DOs**.

All **DIFFERENT**. All **GOOD**.

People who are different often **SOLVE PROBLEMS** differently. They become **VALUABLE PROBLEM SOLVERS**.

all sorts of problems

in space

medical research

the environment

peace keeping

Different is **NOT BAD**.
In fact, different is GOOD,
to be **PRIZED**.
Different is the **WORLD**.

How *boring* it would be if we were all the same!